MY NAME

....

....

COPYRIGHT © GET FIT NOTEBOOKS
THIS PUBLICATION IS PROTECTED BY COPYRIGHT.
ALL RIGHTS RESERVED. NO PART OF THIS PUBLICATION MAY BE REPRODUCED OR TRANSMITTED IN ANY FORM OR BY ANY MEANS, ELECTRONIC OR MECHANICAL, INCLUDING PHOTOCOPYING, RECORDING, OR ANY OTHER INFORMATION STORAGE AND RETRIEVAL SYSTEM, WITHOUT THE WRITTEN PERMISSION FROM THE COPYRIGHT OWNER. FOR INFORMATION, PLEASE WRITE TO: INFO@STUDIO5519.COM

ISBN-13: 978-1545378489
ISBN-10: 1545378487

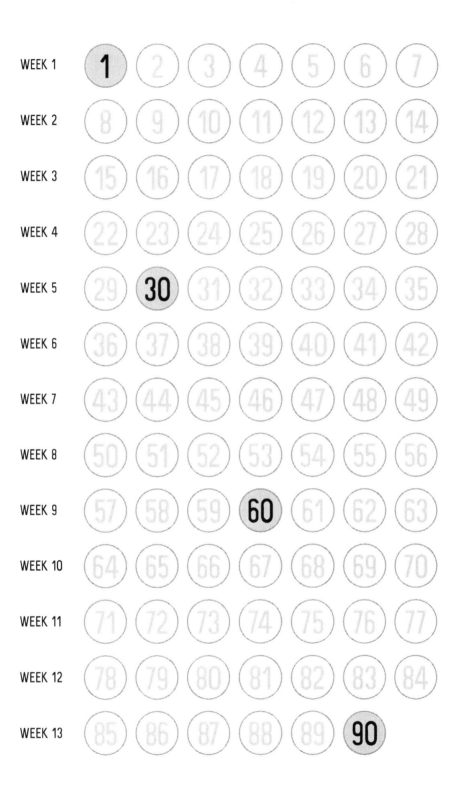

DAY 1

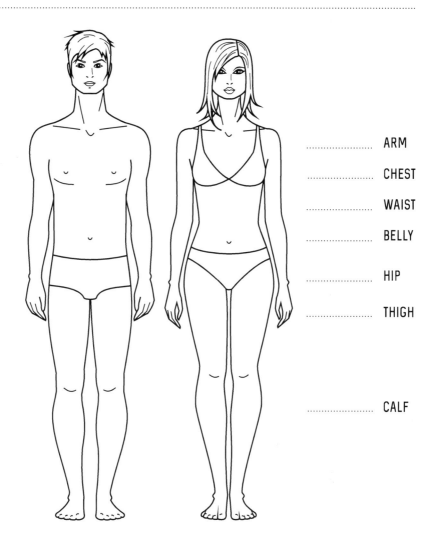

.... ARM
.... CHEST
.... WAIST
.... BELLY
.... HIP
.... THIGH

.... CALF

WEIGHT

BMI

DAY (1)

MO TU WE TH FR SA SU

DATE ....

HOW I FEEL

BREAKFAST | LUNCH | DINNER

SNACKS

TOTAL CALORIES

WEIGHT   SLEEP   WATER   PROTEIN

PROTEIN CONTENT   FIBER CONTENT

OTHER

♥ **RUNS & EXERCISE / OTHER ACTIVITIES** | SET / REPS / DISTANCE | TIME

NOTES

6A 7 8 9 10 11 12P 1 2 3 4 5 6 7 8 9 10+

B=BREAKFAST   L=LUNCH   D=DINNER   S=SNACKS   R=RUN   E=EXERCISE

HOW I FEEL

MO TU WE TH FR SA SU

DATE ....

DAY 2

BREAKFAST

....
....
....
....
....
....

SNACKS

....
....
....

TOTAL CALORIES

_____

PROTEIN CONTENT   FIBER CONTENT

OTHER

....

LUNCH

....
....
....
....
....
....
....
....
....
....

DINNER

....
....
....
....
....
....
....
....
....
....

WEIGHT   SLEEP   WATER   PROTEIN

RUNS & EXERCISE / OTHER ACTIVITIES   SET / REPS / DISTANCE   TIME

....
....
....
....
....

NOTES

....
....

6A 7 8 9 10 11 12P 1 2 3 4 5 6 7 8 9 10+

B=BREAKFAST L=LUNCH D=DINNER S=SNACKS R=RUN E=EXERCISE

DAY 3

MO TU WE TH FR SA SU

DATE ....

HOW I FEEL

○ ○ ○ ○

BREAKFAST

LUNCH

DINNER

SNACKS

TOTAL CALORIES

PROTEIN CONTENT   FIBER CONTENT

OTHER

WEIGHT   SLEEP   WATER   PROTEIN

♥ RUNS & EXERCISE / OTHER ACTIVITIES   SET / REPS / DISTANCE   TIME

NOTES

🕐   6A 7 8 9 10 11 12P 1 2 3 4 5 6 7 8 9 10+

B=BREAKFAST   L=LUNCH   D=DINNER   S=SNACKS   R=RUN   E=EXERCISE

HOW I FEEL

MO TU WE TH FR SA SU

DATE ....

DAY 4

BREAKFAST

LUNCH

DINNER

SNACKS

TOTAL CALORIES

PROTEIN CONTENT   FIBER CONTENT

WEIGHT

SLEEP

WATER

PROTEIN

OTHER

RUNS & EXERCISE / OTHER ACTIVITIES   SET / REPS / DISTANCE   TIME

NOTES

6A 7 8 9 10 11 12P 1 2 3 4 5 6 7 8 9 10+

B=BREAKFAST   L=LUNCH   D=DINNER   S=SNACKS   R=RUN   E=EXERCISE

DAY (5)

MO TU WE TH FR SA SU

DATE ....

HOW I FEEL

BREAKFAST

LUNCH

DINNER

SNACKS

TOTAL CALORIES

PROTEIN CONTENT FIBER CONTENT

WEIGHT

SLEEP

WATER

PROTEIN

OTHER

♥ RUNS & EXERCISE / OTHER ACTIVITIES | SET / REPS / DISTANCE | TIME

NOTES

6A 7 8 9 10 11 12P 1 2 3 4 5 6 7 8 9 10+

B=BREAKFAST L=LUNCH D=DINNER S=SNACKS R=RUN E=EXERCISE

HOW I FEEL

MO TU WE TH FR SA SU

DATE ....

DAY 6

BREAKFAST

LUNCH

DINNER

SNACKS

TOTAL CALORIES

PROTEIN CONTENT   FIBER CONTENT

WEIGHT   SLEEP   WATER   PROTEIN

OTHER

RUNS & EXERCISE / OTHER ACTIVITIES   SET / REPS / DISTANCE   TIME

NOTES

6A 7 8 9 10 11 12P 1 2 3 4 5 6 7 8 9 10+

B=BREAKFAST   L=LUNCH   D=DINNER   S=SNACKS   R=RUN   E=EXERCISE

DAY (7)

MO TU WE TH FR SA SU

DATE ....

HOW I FEEL

○   ○   ○   ○

BREAKFAST

....
....
....
....
....

SNACKS

....
....
....
....

——————   ——————

TOTAL CALORIES

——————   ——————
PROTEIN CONTENT   FIBER CONTENT

——————   ——————

OTHER

....

LUNCH

....
....
....
....
....
....
....
....
....
....
....

DINNER

....
....
....
....
....
....
....
....
....
....
....

WEIGHT   SLEEP   WATER   PROTEIN

♡ **RUNS & EXERCISE / OTHER ACTIVITIES**   **SET / REPS / DISTANCE**   **TIME**

....
....
....
....
....

NOTES

....
....

🕐   6A   7   8   9   10   11   12P   1   2   3   4   5   6   7   8   9   10+

B=BREAKFAST   L=LUNCH   D=DINNER   S=SNACKS   R=RUN   E=EXERCISE

HOW I FEEL

MO TU WE TH FR SA SU

DATE ....

DAY 8

BREAKFAST

LUNCH

DINNER

SNACKS

TOTAL CALORIES

PROTEIN CONTENT   FIBER CONTENT

WEIGHT   SLEEP   WATER   PROTEIN

OTHER

RUNS & EXERCISE / OTHER ACTIVITIES   SET / REPS / DISTANCE   TIME

NOTES

6A 7 8 9 10 11 12P 1 2 3 4 5 6 7 8 9 10+
B=BREAKFAST   L=LUNCH   D=DINNER   S=SNACKS   R=RUN   E=EXERCISE

DAY 9

MO TU WE TH FR SA SU

DATE ....

HOW I FEEL

☺ ☺ 😐 ☹
○ ○ ○ ○

BREAKFAST

....
....
....
....
....
....

SNACKS

....
....
....
....

TOTAL CALORIES

_____

PROTEIN CONTENT   FIBER CONTENT

_____   _____

OTHER

LUNCH

....
....
....
....
....
....
....
....
....
....
....

DINNER

....
....
....
....
....
....
....
....
....
....
....

WEIGHT   SLEEP   WATER   PROTEIN

_____

....

 RUNS & EXERCISE / OTHER ACTIVITIES

....
....
....
....

SET / REPS / DISTANCE

....
....
....
_____

TIME

....
....
....
_____

NOTES

....
....
....

🕐 6A 7 8 9 10 11 12P 1 2 3 4 5 6 7 8 9 10+

B=BREAKFAST   L=LUNCH   D=DINNER   S=SNACKS   R=RUN   E=EXERCISE

HOW I FEEL

MO TU WE TH FR SA SU

DATE ....

DAY (10)

BREAKFAST

LUNCH

DINNER

SNACKS

TOTAL CALORIES

WEIGHT

SLEEP

WATER

PROTEIN

PROTEIN CONTENT   FIBER CONTENT

OTHER

♥ RUNS & EXERCISE / OTHER ACTIVITIES

SET / REPS / DISTANCE

TIME

NOTES

6A 7 8 9 10 11 12P 1 2 3 4 5 6 7 8 9 10+

B=BREAKFAST   L=LUNCH   D=DINNER   S=SNACKS   R=RUN   E=EXERCISE

DAY (11)

MO TU WE TH FR SA SU

DATE ....

HOW I FEEL

BREAKFAST

....
....
....
....
....

SNACKS

....
....
....

TOTAL CALORIES

_____

PROTEIN CONTENT   FIBER CONTENT

OTHER

....

LUNCH

....
....
....
....
....
....
....
....
....
....

WEIGHT

SLEEP

WATER

PROTEIN

DINNER

....
....
....
....
....
....
....
....

♥ **RUNS & EXERCISE / OTHER ACTIVITIES**   SET / REPS / DISTANCE   TIME

....
....
....
....
....

NOTES

....
....

6A 7 8 9 10 11 12P 1 2 3 4 5 6 7 8 9 10+

B=BREAKFAST   L=LUNCH   D=DINNER   S=SNACKS   R=RUN   E=EXERCISE

HOW I FEEL

MO TU WE TH FR SA SU

DATE ....

DAY 12

BREAKFAST
....
....
....
....
....
....
_____ _____

SNACKS
....
....
....
....
_____ _____

TOTAL CALORIES
_____
_____ _____
PROTEIN CONTENT FIBER CONTENT

OTHER
....

LUNCH
....
....
....
....
....
....
....
....
....
....
....
_____ _____

DINNER
....
....
....
....
....
....
....
....
....
....
....
_____ _____

WEIGHT SLEEP WATER PROTEIN
_____ _____ ....

RUNS & EXERCISE / OTHER ACTIVITIES   SET / REPS / DISTANCE   TIME
....
....
....
....
_____ _____ _____

NOTES
....
....

6A 7 8 9 10 11 12P 1 2 3 4 5 6 7 8 9 10+
B=BREAKFAST L=LUNCH D=DINNER S=SNACKS R=RUN E=EXERCISE

DAY (13)

MO TU WE TH FR SA SU

DATE ....

HOW I FEEL

BREAKFAST

....
....
....
....
....

SNACKS

....
....
....

TOTAL CALORIES

PROTEIN CONTENT   FIBER CONTENT

OTHER
....

LUNCH

....
....
....
....
....
....
....
....
....

WEIGHT

DINNER

....
....
....
....
....
....
....
....
....

SLEEP   **WATER**   **PROTEIN**

RUNS & EXERCISE / OTHER ACTIVITIES   SET / REPS / DISTANCE   TIME

....
....
....
....
....

NOTES

....
....

6A 7 8 9 10 11 12P 1 2 3 4 5 6 7 8 9 10+

B=BREAKFAST   L=LUNCH   D=DINNER   S=SNACKS   R=RUN   E=EXERCISE

HOW I FEEL

MO TU WE TH FR SA SU

DATE ....

DAY (14)

BREAKFAST

....
....
....
....
....

SNACKS

....
....
....

TOTAL CALORIES

_____

PROTEIN CONTENT   FIBER CONTENT

LUNCH

....
....
....
....
....
....
....
....
....

DINNER

....
....
....
....
....
....
....
....
....

WEIGHT   SLEEP   WATER   PROTEIN

OTHER

....

RUNS & EXERCISE / OTHER ACTIVITIES   SET / REPS / DISTANCE   TIME

....
....
....
....
....

NOTES

....

6A 7 8 9 10 11 12P 1 2 3 4 5 6 7 8 9 10+

B=BREAKFAST   L=LUNCH   D=DINNER   S=SNACKS   R=RUN   E=EXERCISE

DAY (15)

MO TU WE TH FR SA SU

DATE ....

HOW I FEEL

BREAKFAST

LUNCH

DINNER

SNACKS

TOTAL CALORIES

WEIGHT

SLEEP

WATER

PROTEIN

PROTEIN CONTENT FIBER CONTENT

OTHER

RUNS & EXERCISE / OTHER ACTIVITIES

SET / REPS / DISTANCE

TIME

NOTES

6A 7 8 9 10 11 12P 1 2 3 4 5 6 7 8 9 10+

B=BREAKFAST   L=LUNCH   D=DINNER   S=SNACKS   R=RUN   E=EXERCISE

HOW I FEEL

MO TU WE TH FR SA SU

DATE ....

DAY (16)

BREAKFAST

LUNCH

DINNER

SNACKS

TOTAL CALORIES

PROTEIN CONTENT   FIBER CONTENT

WEIGHT   SLEEP   WATER   PROTEIN

OTHER

RUNS & EXERCISE / OTHER ACTIVITIES   SET / REPS / DISTANCE   TIME

NOTES

6A 7 8 9 10 11 12P 1 2 3 4 5 6 7 8 9 10+

B=BREAKFAST   L=LUNCH   D=DINNER   S=SNACKS   R=RUN   E=EXERCISE

DAY (17)

MO TU WE TH FR SA SU

DATE ....

HOW I FEEL

BREAKFAST

LUNCH

DINNER

SNACKS

TOTAL CALORIES

WEIGHT

SLEEP

WATER

PROTEIN

PROTEIN CONTENT   FIBER CONTENT

OTHER

RUNS & EXERCISE / OTHER ACTIVITIES

SET / REPS / DISTANCE

TIME

NOTES

6A   7   8   9   10   11   12P   1   2   3   4   5   6   7   8   9   10+

B=BREAKFAST   L=LUNCH   D=DINNER   S=SNACKS   R=RUN   E=EXERCISE

HOW I FEEL

MO TU WE TH FR SA SU

DATE ....

DAY 18

BREAKFAST

LUNCH

DINNER

SNACKS

TOTAL CALORIES

PROTEIN CONTENT   FIBER CONTENT

OTHER

WEIGHT   SLEEP   WATER   PROTEIN

RUNS & EXERCISE / OTHER ACTIVITIES

SET / REPS / DISTANCE

TIME

NOTES

6A 7 8 9 10 11 12P 1 2 3 4 5 6 7 8 9 10+

B=BREAKFAST   L=LUNCH   D=DINNER   S=SNACKS   R=RUN   E=EXERCISE

DAY (19)

MO TU WE TH FR SA SU

DATE ....

HOW I FEEL

BREAKFAST

LUNCH

DINNER

SNACKS

TOTAL CALORIES

WEIGHT

SLEEP

WATER

PROTEIN

PROTEIN CONTENT FIBER CONTENT

OTHER

RUNS & EXERCISE / OTHER ACTIVITIES

SET / REPS / DISTANCE

TIME

NOTES

6A 7 8 9 10 11 12P 1 2 3 4 5 6 7 8 9 10+

B=BREAKFAST L=LUNCH D=DINNER S=SNACKS R=RUN E=EXERCISE

HOW I FEEL

MO TU WE TH FR SA SU

DATE ....

DAY 20

BREAKFAST
....
....
....
....
....
....
——— —— ——

LUNCH
....
....
....
....
....
....
....
....
....
....

DINNER
....
....
....
....
....
....
....
....
....
....

SNACKS
....
....
....
....
——— —— ——

TOTAL CALORIES
———————————
PROTEIN CONTENT   FIBER CONTENT
——————— ————

WEIGHT   SLEEP   WATER   PROTEIN

====

OTHER
....

♡ **RUNS & EXERCISE / OTHER ACTIVITIES**   **SET / REPS / DISTANCE**   **TIME**
....
....
....
....
....
....

NOTES
....
....

🕐 6A 7 8 9 10 11 12P 1 2 3 4 5 6 7 8 9 10+
   B=BREAKFAST   L=LUNCH   D=DINNER   S=SNACKS   R=RUN   E=EXERCISE

DAY (21)

MO TU WE TH FR SA SU

DATE ....

HOW I FEEL

BREAKFAST

LUNCH

DINNER

SNACKS

TOTAL CALORIES

WEIGHT

SLEEP

WATER

PROTEIN

PROTEIN CONTENT FIBER CONTENT

OTHER

♥ RUNS & EXERCISE / OTHER ACTIVITIES

SET / REPS / DISTANCE

TIME

NOTES

6A 7 8 9 10 11 12P 1 2 3 4 5 6 7 8 9 10+

B=BREAKFAST L=LUNCH D=DINNER S=SNACKS R=RUN E=EXERCISE

HOW I FEEL

MO TU WE TH FR SA SU

DATE ....

DAY 22

BREAKFAST

LUNCH

DINNER

SNACKS

TOTAL CALORIES

PROTEIN CONTENT   FIBER CONTENT

WEIGHT   SLEEP   WATER   PROTEIN

OTHER

RUNS & EXERCISE / OTHER ACTIVITIES   SET / REPS / DISTANCE   TIME

NOTES

6A 7 8 9 10 11 12P 1 2 3 4 5 6 7 8 9 10+

B=BREAKFAST   L=LUNCH   D=DINNER   S=SNACKS   R=RUN   E=EXERCISE

DAY (23)

MO TU WE TH FR SA SU

DATE ....

HOW I FEEL

BREAKFAST

LUNCH

DINNER

SNACKS

TOTAL CALORIES

WEIGHT SLEEP WATER PROTEIN

PROTEIN CONTENT FIBER CONTENT

OTHER

RUNS & EXERCISE / OTHER ACTIVITIES SET / REPS / DISTANCE TIME

NOTES

6A 7 8 9 10 11 12P 1 2 3 4 5 6 7 8 9 10+

B=BREAKFAST L=LUNCH D=DINNER S=SNACKS R=RUN E=EXERCISE

HOW I FEEL

MO TU WE TH FR SA SU

DATE ....

DAY 24

BREAKFAST

....
....
....
....
....

SNACKS

....
....
....

TOTAL CALORIES

_____

PROTEIN CONTENT   FIBER CONTENT

OTHER

....

LUNCH

....
....
....
....
....
....
....
....
....

DINNER

....
....
....
....
....
....
....
....
....

WEIGHT   SLEEP   WATER   PROTEIN

RUNS & EXERCISE / OTHER ACTIVITIES   SET / REPS / DISTANCE   TIME

....
....
....
....
....

NOTES

....
....

   6A 7 8 9 10 11 12P 1 2 3 4 5 6 7 8 9 10+

B=BREAKFAST   L=LUNCH   D=DINNER   S=SNACKS   R=RUN   E=EXERCISE

DAY 25

MO TU WE TH FR SA SU

DATE ....

HOW I FEEL
○ ○ ○ ○

BREAKFAST

....
....
....
....
....
....

_____ __ ___

SNACKS

....
....
....
....

_____ __ ___

TOTAL CALORIES

_____ _____
PROTEIN CONTENT FIBER CONTENT

_____ _____
OTHER

LUNCH

....
....
....
....
....
....
....
....
....
....
....
....

DINNER

....
....
....
....
....
....
....
....
....
....
....
....

_____ __ ___

WEIGHT   SLEEP   WATER   PROTEIN

_____   ....

♡ **RUNS & EXERCISE / OTHER ACTIVITIES**   **SET / REPS / DISTANCE**   **TIME**

....
....
....
....
....

                                  _____   _____

NOTES

....
....

🕐 6A 7 8 9 10 11 12P 1 2 3 4 5 6 7 8 9 10+

B=BREAKFAST   L=LUNCH   D=DINNER   S=SNACKS   R=RUN   E=EXERCISE

HOW I FEEL

MO TU WE TH FR SA SU

DATE ....

DAY 26

BREAKFAST

LUNCH

DINNER

SNACKS

TOTAL CALORIES

PROTEIN CONTENT   FIBER CONTENT

WEIGHT   SLEEP   WATER   PROTEIN

OTHER

RUNS & EXERCISE / OTHER ACTIVITIES   SET / REPS / DISTANCE   TIME

NOTES

6A 7 8 9 10 11 12P 1 2 3 4 5 6 7 8 9 10+

B=BREAKFAST   L=LUNCH   D=DINNER   S=SNACKS   R=RUN   E=EXERCISE

DAY (27)

MO TU WE TH FR SA SU

DATE ....

HOW I FEEL

BREAKFAST

LUNCH

DINNER

SNACKS

TOTAL CALORIES

PROTEIN CONTENT   FIBER CONTENT

WEIGHT

SLEEP

WATER

PROTEIN

OTHER

♥ RUNS & EXERCISE / OTHER ACTIVITIES

SET / REPS / DISTANCE

TIME

NOTES

6A 7 8 9 10 11 12P 1 2 3 4 5 6 7 8 9 10+

B=BREAKFAST   L=LUNCH   D=DINNER   S=SNACKS   R=RUN   E=EXERCISE

HOW I FEEL

MO TU WE TH FR SA SU

DATE ....

DAY 28

BREAKFAST

LUNCH

DINNER

SNACKS

TOTAL CALORIES

PROTEIN CONTENT   FIBER CONTENT

WEIGHT   SLEEP   WATER   PROTEIN

OTHER

RUNS & EXERCISE / OTHER ACTIVITIES   SET / REPS / DISTANCE   TIME

NOTES

6A 7 8 9 10 11 12P 1 2 3 4 5 6 7 8 9 10+

B=BREAKFAST   L=LUNCH   D=DINNER   S=SNACKS   R=RUN   E=EXERCISE

DAY (29)

MO TU WE TH FR SA SU

DATE ....

HOW I FEEL

BREAKFAST | LUNCH | DINNER

SNACKS

TOTAL CALORIES

WEIGHT SLEEP WATER PROTEIN

PROTEIN CONTENT FIBER CONTENT

OTHER

♡ RUNS & EXERCISE / OTHER ACTIVITIES | SET / REPS / DISTANCE | TIME

NOTES

6A 7 8 9 10 11 12P 1 2 3 4 5 6 7 8 9 10+

B=BREAKFAST L=LUNCH D=DINNER S=SNACKS R=RUN E=EXERCISE

DAY 30

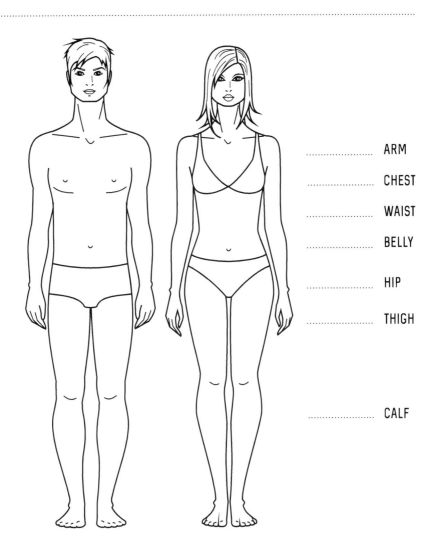

.... ARM
.... CHEST
.... WAIST
.... BELLY
.... HIP
.... THIGH

.... CALF

WEIGHT

BMI

DAY (30)

MO TU WE TH FR SA SU

DATE ....

HOW I FEEL

○ ○ ○ ○

BREAKFAST

....
....
....
....
....

SNACKS

....
....
....

TOTAL CALORIES

_____

PROTEIN CONTENT **FIBER CONTENT**

_____

OTHER

....

LUNCH

....
....
....
....
....
....
....
....
....
....

DINNER

....
....
....
....
....
....
....
....
....
....

WEIGHT **SLEEP** **WATER** **PROTEIN**

_____

♥ **RUNS & EXERCISE / OTHER ACTIVITIES**   **SET / REPS / DISTANCE**   **TIME**

....
....
....
....

NOTES

....
....
....

🕐 6A 7 8 9 10 11 12P 1 2 3 4 5 6 7 8 9 10+

B=BREAKFAST L=LUNCH D=DINNER S=SNACKS R=RUN E=EXERCISE

HOW I FEEL

MO TU WE TH FR SA SU

DATE ....

DAY 31

BREAKFAST | LUNCH | DINNER

SNACKS

TOTAL CALORIES

PROTEIN CONTENT   FIBER CONTENT

WEIGHT   SLEEP   WATER   PROTEIN

OTHER

RUNS & EXERCISE / OTHER ACTIVITIES | SET / REPS / DISTANCE | TIME

NOTES

 6A 7 8 9 10 11 12P 1 2 3 4 5 6 7 8 9 10+

B=BREAKFAST   L=LUNCH   D=DINNER   S=SNACKS   R=RUN   E=EXERCISE

DAY (32)

MO TU WE TH FR SA SU

DATE ....

HOW I FEEL

BREAKFAST

LUNCH

DINNER

SNACKS

TOTAL CALORIES

WEIGHT   SLEEP   WATER   PROTEIN

PROTEIN CONTENT   FIBER CONTENT

OTHER

♡ RUNS & EXERCISE / OTHER ACTIVITIES   SET / REPS / DISTANCE   TIME

NOTES

6A 7 8 9 10 11 12P 1 2 3 4 5 6 7 8 9 10+

B=BREAKFAST   L=LUNCH   D=DINNER   S=SNACKS   R=RUN   E=EXERCISE

HOW I FEEL

MO TU WE TH FR SA SU

DATE ....

DAY (33)

BREAKFAST

LUNCH

DINNER

SNACKS

TOTAL CALORIES

PROTEIN CONTENT   FIBER CONTENT

WEIGHT   SLEEP   WATER   PROTEIN

OTHER

RUNS & EXERCISE / OTHER ACTIVITIES   SET / REPS / DISTANCE   TIME

NOTES

6A 7 8 9 10 11 12P 1 2 3 4 5 6 7 8 9 10+

B=BREAKFAST   L=LUNCH   D=DINNER   S=SNACKS   R=RUN   E=EXERCISE

DAY (34)

MO TU WE TH FR SA SU

DATE ....

HOW I FEEL

BREAKFAST

LUNCH

DINNER

SNACKS

TOTAL CALORIES

WEIGHT   SLEEP   WATER   PROTEIN

PROTEIN CONTENT   FIBER CONTENT

OTHER

♥ RUNS & EXERCISE / OTHER ACTIVITIES   SET / REPS / DISTANCE   TIME

NOTES

6A 7 8 9 10 11 12P 1 2 3 4 5 6 7 8 9 10+

B=BREAKFAST   L=LUNCH   D=DINNER   S=SNACKS   R=RUN   E=EXERCISE

HOW I FEEL

MO TU WE TH FR SA SU

DATE ....

DAY 35

BREAKFAST

LUNCH

DINNER

SNACKS

TOTAL CALORIES

PROTEIN CONTENT   FIBER CONTENT

WEIGHT   SLEEP   WATER   PROTEIN

OTHER

RUNS & EXERCISE / OTHER ACTIVITIES   SET / REPS / DISTANCE   TIME

NOTES

6A 7 8 9 10 11 12P 1 2 3 4 5 6 7 8 9 10+
B=BREAKFAST   L=LUNCH   D=DINNER   S=SNACKS   R=RUN   E=EXERCISE

DAY (36)

MO TU WE TH FR SA SU

DATE ....

HOW I FEEL

BREAKFAST

LUNCH

DINNER

SNACKS

TOTAL CALORIES

WEIGHT | SLEEP | WATER | PROTEIN

PROTEIN CONTENT FIBER CONTENT

OTHER

♡ RUNS & EXERCISE / OTHER ACTIVITIES | SET / REPS / DISTANCE | TIME

NOTES

🕐 6A 7 8 9 10 11 12P 1 2 3 4 5 6 7 8 9 10+

B=BREAKFAST L=LUNCH D=DINNER S=SNACKS R=RUN E=EXERCISE

HOW I FEEL

MO TU WE TH FR SA SU

DATE ....

DAY (37)

BREAKFAST

LUNCH

DINNER

SNACKS

TOTAL CALORIES

PROTEIN CONTENT   FIBER CONTENT

WEIGHT   SLEEP   WATER   PROTEIN

OTHER

RUNS & EXERCISE / OTHER ACTIVITIES   SET / REPS / DISTANCE   TIME

NOTES

6A 7 8 9 10 11 12P 1 2 3 4 5 6 7 8 9 10+

B=BREAKFAST   L=LUNCH   D=DINNER   S=SNACKS   R=RUN   E=EXERCISE

DAY (38)

MO TU WE TH FR SA SU

DATE ....

HOW I FEEL

☺ ☺ 😐 ☹
○ ○ ○ ○

BREAKFAST

LUNCH

DINNER

SNACKS

TOTAL CALORIES
_____ _____
PROTEIN CONTENT FIBER CONTENT
_____ _____
OTHER

WEIGHT   SLEEP   WATER   PROTEIN

♥ RUNS & EXERCISE / OTHER ACTIVITIES

SET / REPS / DISTANCE

TIME

NOTES

🕐 6A 7 8 9 10 11 12P 1 2 3 4 5 6 7 8 9 10+
B=BREAKFAST   L=LUNCH   D=DINNER   S=SNACKS   R=RUN   E=EXERCISE

HOW I FEEL

MO TU WE TH FR SA SU

DATE ....

DAY 39

BREAKFAST

LUNCH

DINNER

SNACKS

TOTAL CALORIES

PROTEIN CONTENT   FIBER CONTENT

WEIGHT   SLEEP   WATER   PROTEIN

OTHER

RUNS & EXERCISE / OTHER ACTIVITIES   SET / REPS / DISTANCE   TIME

NOTES

6A 7 8 9 10 11 12P 1 2 3 4 5 6 7 8 9 10+

B=BREAKFAST   L=LUNCH   D=DINNER   S=SNACKS   R=RUN   E=EXERCISE

DAY (40)

MO TU WE TH FR SA SU

DATE ....

HOW I FEEL

BREAKFAST

LUNCH

DINNER

SNACKS

TOTAL CALORIES

WEIGHT

SLEEP

WATER

PROTEIN

PROTEIN CONTENT   FIBER CONTENT

OTHER

♡ **RUNS & EXERCISE / OTHER ACTIVITIES**   SET / REPS / DISTANCE   TIME

NOTES

6A 7 8 9 10 11 12P 1 2 3 4 5 6 7 8 9 10+

B=BREAKFAST   L=LUNCH   D=DINNER   S=SNACKS   R=RUN   E=EXERCISE

HOW I FEEL

MO TU WE TH FR SA SU

DATE ....

DAY (41)

BREAKFAST

LUNCH

DINNER

SNACKS

TOTAL CALORIES

PROTEIN CONTENT   FIBER CONTENT

WEIGHT   SLEEP   WATER   PROTEIN

OTHER

RUNS & EXERCISE / OTHER ACTIVITIES   SET / REPS / DISTANCE   TIME

NOTES

6A 7 8 9 10 11 12P 1 2 3 4 5 6 7 8 9 10+
B=BREAKFAST   L=LUNCH   D=DINNER   S=SNACKS   R=RUN   E=EXERCISE

DAY 42

MO TU WE TH FR SA SU

DATE ....

HOW I FEEL

BREAKFAST
....
....
....
....
....
....

SNACKS
....
....
....

TOTAL CALORIES
_____
PROTEIN CONTENT   FIBER CONTENT
_____
OTHER

LUNCH
....
....
....
....
....
....
....
....
....
....
....

DINNER
....
....
....
....
....
....
....
....
....
....
....

WEIGHT   SLEEP   WATER   PROTEIN

RUNS & EXERCISE / OTHER ACTIVITIES   SET / REPS / DISTANCE   TIME
....
....
....
....

NOTES
....
....

 6A 7 8 9 10 11 12P 1 2 3 4 5 6 7 8 9 10+

B=BREAKFAST   L=LUNCH   D=DINNER   S=SNACKS   R=RUN   E=EXERCISE

HOW I FEEL

MO TU WE TH FR SA SU

DATE ....

DAY 43

BREAKFAST

LUNCH

DINNER

SNACKS

TOTAL CALORIES

PROTEIN CONTENT   FIBER CONTENT

WEIGHT   SLEEP   WATER   PROTEIN

OTHER

RUNS & EXERCISE / OTHER ACTIVITIES   SET / REPS / DISTANCE   TIME

NOTES

6A 7 8 9 10 11 12P 1 2 3 4 5 6 7 8 9 10+

B=BREAKFAST   L=LUNCH   D=DINNER   S=SNACKS   R=RUN   E=EXERCISE

DAY (44)

MO TU WE TH FR SA SU

DATE ....

HOW I FEEL

BREAKFAST

LUNCH

DINNER

SNACKS

TOTAL CALORIES

WEIGHT

SLEEP

WATER

PROTEIN

PROTEIN CONTENT FIBER CONTENT

OTHER

♥ RUNS & EXERCISE / OTHER ACTIVITIES | SET / REPS / DISTANCE | TIME

NOTES

6A 7 8 9 10 11 12P 1 2 3 4 5 6 7 8 9 10+

B=BREAKFAST   L=LUNCH   D=DINNER   S=SNACKS   R=RUN   E=EXERCISE

HOW I FEEL

MO TU WE TH FR SA SU

DATE ....

DAY (45)

BREAKFAST | LUNCH | DINNER

SNACKS

TOTAL CALORIES

PROTEIN CONTENT   FIBER CONTENT

WEIGHT   SLEEP   WATER   PROTEIN

OTHER

RUNS & EXERCISE / OTHER ACTIVITIES | SET / REPS / DISTANCE | TIME

NOTES

6A 7 8 9 10 11 12P 1 2 3 4 5 6 7 8 9 10+

B=BREAKFAST   L=LUNCH   D=DINNER   S=SNACKS   R=RUN   E=EXERCISE

DAY (46)

MO TU WE TH FR SA SU

DATE ....

HOW I FEEL

○ ○ ○ ○

BREAKFAST

LUNCH

DINNER

SNACKS

TOTAL CALORIES

PROTEIN CONTENT   FIBER CONTENT

WEIGHT   SLEEP   WATER   PROTEIN

OTHER

RUNS & EXERCISE / OTHER ACTIVITIES

SET / REPS / DISTANCE

TIME

NOTES

6A 7 8 9 10 11 12P 1 2 3 4 5 6 7 8 9 10+

B=BREAKFAST   L=LUNCH   D=DINNER   S=SNACKS   R=RUN   E=EXERCISE

HOW I FEEL

MO TU WE TH FR SA SU

DATE ....

DAY (47)

BREAKFAST

....
....
....
....
....
....

————— ——— ———

SNACKS

....
....
....
....

————— ——— ———

TOTAL CALORIES

—————————————————
PROTEIN CONTENT FIBER CONTENT

LUNCH

....
....
....
....
....
....
....
....
....
....
....

DINNER

....
....
....
....
....
....
....
....
....
....
....

WEIGHT   SLEEP   WATER   PROTEIN

—————————   ——————————   ....

OTHER
....

RUNS & EXERCISE / OTHER ACTIVITIES   SET / REPS / DISTANCE   TIME

....
....
....
....
....

NOTES
....
....

6A 7 8 9 10 11 12P 1 2 3 4 5 6 7 8 9 10+

B=BREAKFAST   L=LUNCH   D=DINNER   S=SNACKS   R=RUN   E=EXERCISE

DAY (48)

MO TU WE TH FR SA SU

DATE ....

HOW I FEEL

BREAKFAST

LUNCH

DINNER

SNACKS

TOTAL CALORIES

WEIGHT SLEEP WATER PROTEIN

PROTEIN CONTENT FIBER CONTENT

OTHER

....

♥ RUNS & EXERCISE / OTHER ACTIVITIES   SET / REPS / DISTANCE   TIME

NOTES

....

....

6A 7 8 9 10 11 12P 1 2 3 4 5 6 7 8 9 10+

B=BREAKFAST L=LUNCH D=DINNER S=SNACKS R=RUN E=EXERCISE

HOW I FEEL

MO TU WE TH FR SA SU

DATE ....

DAY 49

BREAKFAST

....
....
....
....
....

_____ ____ ____

SNACKS

....
....
....
....

_____ ____ ____

TOTAL CALORIES

_____

PROTEIN CONTENT   FIBER CONTENT

LUNCH

....
....
....
....
....
....
....
....
....
....
....

DINNER

....
....
....
....
....
....
....
....
....
....
....

WEIGHT   SLEEP   WATER   PROTEIN

_____   _____   ....

OTHER
....

RUNS & EXERCISE / OTHER ACTIVITIES   SET / REPS / DISTANCE   TIME

....
....
....
....
....

NOTES

....
....

6A 7 8 9 10 11 12P 1 2 3 4 5 6 7 8 9 10+

B=BREAKFAST   L=LUNCH   D=DINNER   S=SNACKS   R=RUN   E=EXERCISE

DAY (50)

MO TU WE TH FR SA SU

DATE ....

HOW I FEEL

BREAKFAST

LUNCH

DINNER

SNACKS

TOTAL CALORIES

PROTEIN CONTENT   FIBER CONTENT

WEIGHT   **SLEEP**   **WATER**   **PROTEIN**

OTHER

RUNS & EXERCISE / OTHER ACTIVITIES

SET / REPS / DISTANCE   TIME

NOTES

6A 7 8 9 10 11 12P 1 2 3 4 5 6 7 8 9 10+

B=BREAKFAST   L=LUNCH   D=DINNER   S=SNACKS   R=RUN   E=EXERCISE

HOW I FEEL

MO TU WE TH FR SA SU

DATE ....

DAY 51

BREAKFAST

LUNCH

DINNER

SNACKS

TOTAL CALORIES

PROTEIN CONTENT   FIBER CONTENT

WEIGHT   SLEEP   WATER   PROTEIN

OTHER

RUNS & EXERCISE / OTHER ACTIVITIES   SET / REPS / DISTANCE   TIME

NOTES

6A 7 8 9 10 11 12P 1 2 3 4 5 6 7 8 9 10+

B=BREAKFAST   L=LUNCH   D=DINNER   S=SNACKS   R=RUN   E=EXERCISE

DAY (52)

MO TU WE TH FR SA SU

DATE ....

HOW I FEEL

BREAKFAST

....
....
....
....
....

————— ——— ———

SNACKS

....
....
....

LUNCH

....
....
....
....
....
....
....
....
....

————— ——— ———

DINNER

....
....
....
....
....
....
....
....

TOTAL CALORIES

—————————————

PROTEIN CONTENT FIBER CONTENT

————— —————

OTHER

....

WEIGHT   **SLEEP**   **WATER**   **PROTEIN**

———————— ....

RUNS & EXERCISE / OTHER ACTIVITIES   SET / REPS / DISTANCE   TIME

....
....
....
....
....

————————— —————

NOTES

....
....

6A 7 8 9 10 11 12P 1 2 3 4 5 6 7 8 9 10+

B=BREAKFAST   L=LUNCH   D=DINNER   S=SNACKS   R=RUN   E=EXERCISE

HOW I FEEL

MO TU WE TH FR SA SU

DATE ....

DAY 53

BREAKFAST

LUNCH

DINNER

SNACKS

TOTAL CALORIES

PROTEIN CONTENT   FIBER CONTENT

WEIGHT   SLEEP   WATER   PROTEIN

OTHER

RUNS & EXERCISE / OTHER ACTIVITIES   SET / REPS / DISTANCE   TIME

NOTES

6A 7 8 9 10 11 12P 1 2 3 4 5 6 7 8 9 10+

B=BREAKFAST L=LUNCH D=DINNER S=SNACKS R=RUN E=EXERCISE

DAY 54

MO TU WE TH FR SA SU

DATE ....

HOW I FEEL

BREAKFAST

LUNCH

DINNER

SNACKS

TOTAL CALORIES

PROTEIN CONTENT   FIBER CONTENT

WEIGHT

SLEEP

WATER

PROTEIN

OTHER

RUNS & EXERCISE / OTHER ACTIVITIES

SET / REPS / DISTANCE

TIME

NOTES

6A 7 8 9 10 11 12P 1 2 3 4 5 6 7 8 9 10+

B=BREAKFAST   L=LUNCH   D=DINNER   S=SNACKS   R=RUN   E=EXERCISE

HOW I FEEL

MO TU WE TH FR SA SU

DATE ....

DAY 55

BREAKFAST

LUNCH

DINNER

SNACKS

TOTAL CALORIES

PROTEIN CONTENT   FIBER CONTENT

WEIGHT   SLEEP   WATER   PROTEIN

OTHER

RUNS & EXERCISE / OTHER ACTIVITIES   SET / REPS / DISTANCE   TIME

NOTES

6A 7 8 9 10 11 12P 1 2 3 4 5 6 7 8 9 10+

B=BREAKFAST   L=LUNCH   D=DINNER   S=SNACKS   R=RUN   E=EXERCISE

DAY (56)

MO TU WE TH FR SA SU

DATE ....

HOW I FEEL

BREAKFAST

....
....
....
....
....

SNACKS

....
....
....

TOTAL CALORIES

PROTEIN CONTENT FIBER CONTENT

OTHER

....

LUNCH

....
....
....
....
....
....
....
....
....
....

WEIGHT

SLEEP

WATER

PROTEIN

DINNER

....
....
....
....
....
....
....
....
....
....

♡ **RUNS & EXERCISE / OTHER ACTIVITIES**   SET / REPS / DISTANCE   TIME

....
....
....
....
....

NOTES

....
....

6A 7 8 9 10 11 12P 1 2 3 4 5 6 7 8 9 10+

B=BREAKFAST   L=LUNCH   D=DINNER   S=SNACKS   R=RUN   E=EXERCISE

HOW I FEEL

MO TU WE TH FR SA SU

DATE ....

DAY 57

BREAKFAST

LUNCH

DINNER

SNACKS

TOTAL CALORIES

PROTEIN CONTENT FIBER CONTENT

WEIGHT SLEEP WATER PROTEIN

OTHER

RUNS & EXERCISE / OTHER ACTIVITIES   SET / REPS / DISTANCE   TIME

NOTES

6A 7 8 9 10 11 12P 1 2 3 4 5 6 7 8 9 10+

B=BREAKFAST L=LUNCH D=DINNER S=SNACKS R=RUN E=EXERCISE

DAY (58)

MO TU WE TH FR SA SU

DATE ....

HOW I FEEL

BREAKFAST

LUNCH

DINNER

SNACKS

TOTAL CALORIES

PROTEIN CONTENT   FIBER CONTENT

WEIGHT   SLEEP   WATER   PROTEIN

OTHER

RUNS & EXERCISE / OTHER ACTIVITIES

SET / REPS / DISTANCE   TIME

NOTES

6A 7 8 9 10 11 12P 1 2 3 4 5 6 7 8 9 10+

B=BREAKFAST   L=LUNCH   D=DINNER   S=SNACKS   R=RUN   E=EXERCISE

HOW I FEEL

MO TU WE TH FR SA SU

DATE ....

DAY (59)

BREAKFAST
....
....
....
....
....
....
——————

SNACKS
....
....
....
——— ———

TOTAL CALORIES
————————
PROTEIN CONTENT   FIBER CONTENT

LUNCH
....
....
....
....
....
....
....
....
....
....
....
——— ———

DINNER
....
....
....
....
....
....
....
....
....
....
....
——— ———

WEIGHT   SLEEP   WATER   PROTEIN
======== ....

OTHER
....

RUNS & EXERCISE / OTHER ACTIVITIES
....
....
....
....
....

SET / REPS / DISTANCE
....
....
....
....
....

TIME
....
....
....
....
....

NOTES
....
....

6A 7 8 9 10 11 12P 1 2 3 4 5 6 7 8 9 10+
B=BREAKFAST   L=LUNCH   D=DINNER   S=SNACKS   R=RUN   E=EXERCISE

DAY 60

ARM ....

CHEST ....

WAIST ....

BELLY ....

HIP ....

THIGH ....

CALF ....

WEIGHT

BMI ....

HOW I FEEL

MO TU WE TH FR SA SU

DATE ....

DAY 60

BREAKFAST

LUNCH

DINNER

SNACKS

TOTAL CALORIES

PROTEIN CONTENT   FIBER CONTENT

WEIGHT   SLEEP   WATER   PROTEIN

OTHER

RUNS & EXERCISE / OTHER ACTIVITIES   SET / REPS / DISTANCE   TIME

NOTES

6A 7 8 9 10 11 12P 1 2 3 4 5 6 7 8 9 10+
B=BREAKFAST   L=LUNCH   D=DINNER   S=SNACKS   R=RUN   E=EXERCISE

DAY 61

MO TU WE TH FR SA SU

DATE ....

HOW I FEEL

BREAKFAST

....
....
....
....
....

_____ _____ _____

SNACKS

....
....
....
....

LUNCH

....
....
....
....
....
....
....
....
....
....

DINNER

....
....
....
....
....
....
....
....
....
....

TOTAL CALORIES

_____

PROTEIN CONTENT   FIBER CONTENT

_____   _____

OTHER

WEIGHT **SLEEP** **WATER** **PROTEIN**

....

RUNS & EXERCISE / OTHER ACTIVITIES | **SET / REPS / DISTANCE** | **TIME**

.... | .... | ....
.... | .... | ....
.... | .... | ....
.... | .... | ....

NOTES

....
....

6A 7 8 9 10 11 12P 1 2 3 4 5 6 7 8 9 10+

B=BREAKFAST   L=LUNCH   D=DINNER   S=SNACKS   R=RUN   E=EXERCISE

HOW I FEEL

MO TU WE TH FR SA SU

DATE ....

DAY (62)

BREAKFAST

....
....
....
....
....
....
_____ ____ ____

SNACKS

....
....
....
....

LUNCH

....
....
....
....
....
....
....
....
....
....
....

DINNER

....
....
....
....
....
....
....
....
....
....
....

TOTAL CALORIES

_____

PROTEIN CONTENT   FIBER CONTENT
_____ _____

WEIGHT   SLEEP   WATER   PROTEIN

....

OTHER
....

RUNS & EXERCISE / OTHER ACTIVITIES   SET / REPS / DISTANCE   TIME

....
....
....
....
....

NOTES
....
....

6A 7 8 9 10 11 12P 1 2 3 4 5 6 7 8 9 10+

B=BREAKFAST   L=LUNCH   D=DINNER   S=SNACKS   R=RUN   E=EXERCISE

DAY (63)

MO TU WE TH FR SA SU

DATE ....

HOW I FEEL

😀 🙂 😐 ☹
○ ○ ○ ○

BREAKFAST

....
....
....
....
....
....

SNACKS

....
....
....
....

TOTAL CALORIES

_____ _____
PROTEIN CONTENT FIBER CONTENT

OTHER

....

LUNCH

....
....
....
....
....
....
....
....
....
....
....
....

_____ _____

WEIGHT   SLEEP   WATER   PROTEIN

....

DINNER

....
....
....
....
....
....
....
....
....
....
....
....

....

♡ RUNS & EXERCISE / OTHER ACTIVITIES   SET / REPS / DISTANCE   TIME

....
....
....
....

NOTES

....
....

  6A 7 8 9 10 11 12P 1 2 3 4 5 6 7 8 9 10+

B=BREAKFAST   L=LUNCH   D=DINNER   S=SNACKS   R=RUN   E=EXERCISE

HOW I FEEL

MO TU WE TH FR SA SU

DATE ....

DAY 64

BREAKFAST

LUNCH

DINNER

SNACKS

TOTAL CALORIES

PROTEIN CONTENT   FIBER CONTENT

WEIGHT   SLEEP   WATER   PROTEIN

OTHER

RUNS & EXERCISE / OTHER ACTIVITIES   SET / REPS / DISTANCE   TIME

NOTES

6A 7 8 9 10 11 12P 1 2 3 4 5 6 7 8 9 10+
B=BREAKFAST   L=LUNCH   D=DINNER   S=SNACKS   R=RUN   E=EXERCISE

DAY 65

MO TU WE TH FR SA SU

DATE ....

HOW I FEEL

😀 🙂 😐 ☹
○ ○ ○ ○

BREAKFAST	LUNCH	DINNER
....	....	....
....	....	....
....	....	....
....	....	....
....	....	....

____ ____ ____

SNACKS

.... | .... | ....
.... | .... | ....
.... | .... | ....

____ ____ ____   ____ ____   ____ ____

TOTAL CALIORIES

____ ____
PROTEIN CONTENT   FIBER CONTENT

WEIGHT   SLEEP   WATER   PROTEIN

____ ____ ____ ____

OTHER

....

♡ **RUNS & EXERCISE / OTHER ACTIVITIES**   SET / REPS / DISTANCE   TIME

....	....	....
....	....	....
....	....	....
....	....	....
....	....	....

NOTES

....
....

   6A   7   8   9   10   11   12P   1   2   3   4   5   6   7   8   9   10+

B=BREAKFAST   L=LUNCH   D=DINNER   S=SNACKS   R=RUN   E=EXERCISE

HOW I FEEL

MO TU WE TH FR SA SU

DATE ....

DAY 66

BREAKFAST

LUNCH

DINNER

SNACKS

TOTAL CALORIES

PROTEIN CONTENT   FIBER CONTENT

WEIGHT   SLEEP   WATER   PROTEIN

OTHER

RUNS & EXERCISE / OTHER ACTIVITIES   SET / REPS / DISTANCE   TIME

NOTES

6A 7 8 9 10 11 12P 1 2 3 4 5 6 7 8 9 10+

B=BREAKFAST   L=LUNCH   D=DINNER   S=SNACKS   R=RUN   E=EXERCISE

DAY (67)　　MO TU WE TH FR SA SU

DATE ....

HOW I FEEL

BREAKFAST
....
....
....
....
....
_____ _____

SNACKS
....
....
....

_____ _____ _____

TOTAL CALORIES

_____ _____
PROTEIN CONTENT FIBER CONTENT

_____
OTHER
....

LUNCH
....
....
....
....
....
....
....
....
....
....

DINNER
....
....
....
....
....
....
....
....
....
....

WEIGHT　SLEEP　WATER　PROTEIN

_____ ....

❤ RUNS & EXERCISE / OTHER ACTIVITIES　　SET / REPS / DISTANCE　　TIME

....　..........................　..........................
....　..........................　..........................
....　..........................　..........................
....　..........................　..........................
....　..........................　..........................

NOTES
....
....

 6A 7 8 9 10 11 12P 1 2 3 4 5 6 7 8 9 10+

B=BREAKFAST   L=LUNCH   D=DINNER   S=SNACKS   R=RUN   E=EXERCISE

HOW I FEEL

MO TU WE TH FR SA SU

DATE ....

DAY 68

BREAKFAST

LUNCH

DINNER

SNACKS

TOTAL CALORIES

PROTEIN CONTENT   FIBER CONTENT

WEIGHT   SLEEP   WATER   PROTEIN

OTHER

RUNS & EXERCISE / OTHER ACTIVITIES   SET / REPS / DISTANCE   TIME

NOTES

6A 7 8 9 10 11 12P 1 2 3 4 5 6 7 8 9 10+

B=BREAKFAST   L=LUNCH   D=DINNER   S=SNACKS   R=RUN   E=EXERCISE

DAY (69)

MO TU WE TH FR SA SU

DATE ....

HOW I FEEL

BREAKFAST

LUNCH

DINNER

SNACKS

TOTAL CALORIES

WEIGHT

SLEEP

WATER

PROTEIN

PROTEIN CONTENT FIBER CONTENT

OTHER

RUNS & EXERCISE / OTHER ACTIVITIES

SET / REPS / DISTANCE

TIME

NOTES

6A 7 8 9 10 11 12P 1 2 3 4 5 6 7 8 9 10+

B=BREAKFAST L=LUNCH D=DINNER S=SNACKS R=RUN E=EXERCISE

HOW I FEEL

MO TU WE TH FR SA SU

DATE ....

DAY 70

BREAKFAST

LUNCH

DINNER

SNACKS

TOTAL CALORIES

PROTEIN CONTENT   FIBER CONTENT

WEIGHT   SLEEP   WATER   PROTEIN

OTHER

RUNS & EXERCISE / OTHER ACTIVITIES   SET / REPS / DISTANCE   TIME

NOTES

6A 7 8 9 10 11 12P 1 2 3 4 5 6 7 8 9 10+

B=BREAKFAST   L=LUNCH   D=DINNER   S=SNACKS   R=RUN   E=EXERCISE

DAY (71)

MO TU WE TH FR SA SU

DATE

HOW I FEEL

BREAKFAST

LUNCH

DINNER

SNACKS

TOTAL CALORIES

WEIGHT

SLEEP

WATER

PROTEIN

PROTEIN CONTENT   FIBER CONTENT

OTHER

♡ RUNS & EXERCISE / OTHER ACTIVITIES   SET / REPS / DISTANCE   TIME

NOTES

6A 7 8 9 10 11 12P 1 2 3 4 5 6 7 8 9 10+

B=BREAKFAST   L=LUNCH   D=DINNER   S=SNACKS   R=RUN   E=EXERCISE

HOW I FEEL

MO TU WE TH FR SA SU

DATE ....

DAY 72

BREAKFAST

LUNCH

DINNER

SNACKS

TOTAL CALORIES

PROTEIN CONTENT   FIBER CONTENT

WEIGHT   SLEEP   WATER   PROTEIN

OTHER

RUNS & EXERCISE / OTHER ACTIVITIES   SET / REPS / DISTANCE   TIME

NOTES

6A 7 8 9 10 11 12P 1 2 3 4 5 6 7 8 9 10+

B=BREAKFAST L=LUNCH D=DINNER S=SNACKS R=RUN E=EXERCISE

DAY (73)

MO TU WE TH FR SA SU

DATE ....

HOW I FEEL

BREAKFAST

LUNCH

DINNER

SNACKS

TOTAL CALORIES

PROTEIN CONTENT FIBER CONTENT

WEIGHT

SLEEP

WATER

PROTEIN

OTHER

♡ **RUNS & EXERCISE / OTHER ACTIVITIES**   SET / REPS / DISTANCE   TIME

NOTES

6A 7 8 9 10 11 12P 1 2 3 4 5 6 7 8 9 10+

B=BREAKFAST   L=LUNCH   D=DINNER   S=SNACKS   R=RUN   E=EXERCISE

HOW I FEEL

MO TU WE TH FR SA SU

DATE ....

DAY 74

BREAKFAST

LUNCH

DINNER

SNACKS

TOTAL CALORIES

PROTEIN CONTENT   FIBER CONTENT

WEIGHT   SLEEP   WATER   PROTEIN

OTHER

RUNS & EXERCISE / OTHER ACTIVITIES   SET / REPS / DISTANCE   TIME

NOTES

6A 7 8 9 10 11 12P 1 2 3 4 5 6 7 8 9 10+

B=BREAKFAST   L=LUNCH   D=DINNER   S=SNACKS   R=RUN   E=EXERCISE

DAY 75

MO TU WE TH FR SA SU

DATE ....

HOW I FEEL

BREAKFAST
....
....
....
....
....

SNACKS
....
....
....

TOTAL CALORIES
_____

PROTEIN CONTENT   FIBER CONTENT

OTHER
....

LUNCH
....
....
....
....
....
....
....
....
....
....
....

DINNER
....
....
....
....
....

WEIGHT   SLEEP   WATER   PROTEIN

RUNS & EXERCISE / OTHER ACTIVITIES
....
....
....
....
....

SET / REPS / DISTANCE
....
....
....
....
....

TIME
....
....
....
....
....

NOTES
....
....

6A 7 8 9 10 11 12P 1 2 3 4 5 6 7 8 9 10+

B=BREAKFAST   L=LUNCH   D=DINNER   S=SNACKS   R=RUN   E=EXERCISE

HOW I FEEL

MO TU WE TH FR SA SU

DATE ....

DAY 76

BREAKFAST

LUNCH

DINNER

SNACKS

TOTAL CALORIES

PROTEIN CONTENT   FIBER CONTENT

WEIGHT

SLEEP

WATER

PROTEIN

OTHER

RUNS & EXERCISE / OTHER ACTIVITIES

SET / REPS / DISTANCE

TIME

NOTES

6A 7 8 9 10 11 12P 1 2 3 4 5 6 7 8 9 10+

B=BREAKFAST   L=LUNCH   D=DINNER   S=SNACKS   R=RUN   E=EXERCISE

DAY (77)

MO TU WE TH FR SA SU

DATE ....

HOW I FEEL

BREAKFAST

LUNCH

DINNER

SNACKS

TOTAL CALORIES

WEIGHT

SLEEP

WATER

PROTEIN

PROTEIN CONTENT   FIBER CONTENT

OTHER

♡ RUNS & EXERCISE / OTHER ACTIVITIES

SET / REPS / DISTANCE

TIME

NOTES

6A 7 8 9 10 11 12P 1 2 3 4 5 6 7 8 9 10+

B=BREAKFAST   L=LUNCH   D=DINNER   S=SNACKS   R=RUN   E=EXERCISE

HOW I FEEL

MO TU WE TH FR SA SU

DATE ....

DAY 78

BREAKFAST

LUNCH

DINNER

SNACKS

TOTAL CALORIES

PROTEIN CONTENT   FIBER CONTENT

WEIGHT   SLEEP   WATER   PROTEIN

OTHER

 RUNS & EXERCISE / OTHER ACTIVITIES   SET / REPS / DISTANCE   TIME

NOTES

6A 7 8 9 10 11 12P 1 2 3 4 5 6 7 8 9 10+
B=BREAKFAST   L=LUNCH   D=DINNER   S=SNACKS   R=RUN   E=EXERCISE

DAY (79)

MO TU WE TH FR SA SU

DATE ....

HOW I FEEL

BREAKFAST | LUNCH | DINNER

SNACKS

TOTAL CALORIES

PROTEIN CONTENT   FIBER CONTENT

WEIGHT   SLEEP   WATER   PROTEIN

OTHER

RUNS & EXERCISE / OTHER ACTIVITIES | SET / REPS / DISTANCE | TIME

NOTES

6A 7 8 9 10 11 12P 1 2 3 4 5 6 7 8 9 10+
B=BREAKFAST   L=LUNCH   D=DINNER   S=SNACKS   R=RUN   E=EXERCISE

HOW I FEEL

MO TU WE TH FR SA SU

DATE ....

DAY 80

BREAKFAST	LUNCH	DINNER

SNACKS

TOTAL CALORIES

WEIGHT

SLEEP

WATER

PROTEIN

PROTEIN CONTENT   FIBER CONTENT

OTHER

RUNS & EXERCISE / OTHER ACTIVITIES

	SET / REPS / DISTANCE	TIME

NOTES

6A 7 8 9 10 11 12P 1 2 3 4 5 6 7 8 9 10+

B=BREAKFAST   L=LUNCH   D=DINNER   S=SNACKS   R=RUN   E=EXERCISE

DAY (81)

MO TU WE TH FR SA SU

DATE ....

HOW I FEEL

BREAKFAST	LUNCH	DINNER

SNACKS

TOTAL CALORIES

WEIGHT   **SLEEP**   **WATER**   **PROTEIN**

PROTEIN CONTENT   FIBER CONTENT

OTHER

RUNS & EXERCISE / OTHER ACTIVITIES   SET / REPS / DISTANCE   TIME

NOTES

6A 7 8 9 10 11 12P 1 2 3 4 5 6 7 8 9 10+

B=BREAKFAST   L=LUNCH   D=DINNER   S=SNACKS   R=RUN   E=EXERCISE

HOW I FEEL

MO TU WE TH FR SA SU

DATE ....

DAY (82)

BREAKFAST

LUNCH

DINNER

SNACKS

TOTAL CALORIES

PROTEIN CONTENT   FIBER CONTENT

WEIGHT   SLEEP   WATER   PROTEIN

OTHER

RUNS & EXERCISE / OTHER ACTIVITIES   SET / REPS / DISTANCE   TIME

NOTES

6A 7 8 9 10 11 12P 1 2 3 4 5 6 7 8 9 10+
B=BREAKFAST   L=LUNCH   D=DINNER   S=SNACKS   R=RUN   E=EXERCISE

DAY (83)   MO TU WE TH FR SA SU   HOW I FEEL

DATE ....

BREAKFAST   LUNCH   DINNER

SNACKS

TOTAL CALORIES   WEIGHT   SLEEP   WATER   PROTEIN

PROTEIN CONTENT   FIBER CONTENT

OTHER

RUNS & EXERCISE / OTHER ACTIVITIES   SET / REPS / DISTANCE   TIME

NOTES

6A 7 8 9 10 11 12P 1 2 3 4 5 6 7 8 9 10+
B=BREAKFAST   L=LUNCH   D=DINNER   S=SNACKS   R=RUN   E=EXERCISE

HOW I FEEL

MO TU WE TH FR SA SU

DATE ....

DAY 84

BREAKFAST

....
....
....
....
....
....
_____ _____

SNACKS

....
....
....
_____ _____

TOTAL CALORIES

_____
PROTEIN CONTENT   FIBER CONTENT

LUNCH

....
....
....
....
....
....
....
....
....
....
_____ _____

DINNER

....
....
....
....
....
....
_____ _____

WEIGHT   SLEEP   WATER   PROTEIN

_____   _____   ....

OTHER
....

RUNS & EXERCISE / OTHER ACTIVITIES   SET / REPS / DISTANCE   TIME

....
....
....
....
....

NOTES
....
....
....

6A 7 8 9 10 11 12P 1 2 3 4 5 6 7 8 9 10+
B=BREAKFAST   L=LUNCH   D=DINNER   S=SNACKS   R=RUN   E=EXERCISE

DAY 85

MO TU WE TH FR SA SU

DATE ....

HOW I FEEL
😀 🙂 😐 🙁
○ ○ ○ ○

BREAKFAST
....
....
....
....
....
....
————— ————— —————

SNACKS
....
....
....
....

LUNCH
....
....
....
....
....
....
....
....
....
....

DINNER
....
....
....
....
....
....

————— ————— —————

TOTAL CALORIES
—————
PROTEIN CONTENT   FIBER CONTENT

WEIGHT   **SLEEP**   **WATER**   **PROTEIN**

—————
OTHER
....

 RUNS & EXERCISE / OTHER ACTIVITIES   **SET / REPS / DISTANCE**   **TIME**

....
....
....
....
....

NOTES
....
....

🕐 6A 7 8 9 10 11 12P 1 2 3 4 5 6 7 8 9 10+
B=BREAKFAST   L=LUNCH   D=DINNER   S=SNACKS   R=RUN   E=EXERCISE

HOW I FEEL

MO TU WE TH FR SA SU

DATE ....

DAY 86

BREAKFAST

LUNCH

DINNER

SNACKS

TOTAL CALORIES

PROTEIN CONTENT   FIBER CONTENT

WEIGHT   SLEEP   WATER   PROTEIN

OTHER

RUNS & EXERCISE / OTHER ACTIVITIES   SET / REPS / DISTANCE   TIME

NOTES

6A 7 8 9 10 11 12P 1 2 3 4 5 6 7 8 9 10+

B=BREAKFAST   L=LUNCH   D=DINNER   S=SNACKS   R=RUN   E=EXERCISE

DAY (87)

MO TU WE TH FR SA SU

DATE ....

HOW I FEEL

BREAKFAST	LUNCH	DINNER

SNACKS

TOTAL CALORIES

WEIGHT   SLEEP   WATER   PROTEIN

PROTEIN CONTENT FIBER CONTENT

OTHER

❤ RUNS & EXERCISE / OTHER ACTIVITIES   SET / REPS / DISTANCE   TIME

NOTES

6A 7 8 9 10 11 12P 1 2 3 4 5 6 7 8 9 10+

B=BREAKFAST L=LUNCH D=DINNER S=SNACKS R=RUN E=EXERCISE

HOW I FEEL

MO TU WE TH FR SA SU

DATE ....

DAY 88

BREAKFAST

LUNCH

DINNER

SNACKS

TOTAL CALORIES

PROTEIN CONTENT   FIBER CONTENT

WEIGHT

SLEEP

WATER

PROTEIN

OTHER

RUNS & EXERCISE / OTHER ACTIVITIES

SET / REPS / DISTANCE

TIME

NOTES

6A 7 8 9 10 11 12P 1 2 3 4 5 6 7 8 9 10+

B=BREAKFAST   L=LUNCH   D=DINNER   S=SNACKS   R=RUN   E=EXERCISE

DAY 89

MO TU WE TH FR SA SU

DATE ....

HOW I FEEL

BREAKFAST	LUNCH	DINNER
....	....	....
....	....	....
....	....	....
....	....	....
....	....	....

SNACKS

....

....

....

TOTAL CALORIES

PROTEIN CONTENT   FIBER CONTENT

WEIGHT   SLEEP   WATER   PROTEIN

OTHER

....

RUNS & EXERCISE / OTHER ACTIVITIES | SET / REPS / DISTANCE | TIME

....

NOTES

....

....

6A 7 8 9 10 11 12P 1 2 3 4 5 6 7 8 9 10+

B=BREAKFAST L=LUNCH D=DINNER S=SNACKS R=RUN E=EXERCISE

HOW I FEEL

MO TU WE TH FR SA SU

DATE ....

DAY 90

BREAKFAST
....
....
....
....
....
....

SNACKS
....
....
....

TOTAL CALORIES
_____
PROTEIN CONTENT   FIBER CONTENT

LUNCH
....
....
....
....
....
....
....
....
....
....

DINNER
....
....
....
....
....
....
....
....
....
....

WEIGHT   SLEEP   WATER   PROTEIN

OTHER
....

RUNS & EXERCISE / OTHER ACTIVITIES   SET / REPS / DISTANCE   TIME
....
....
....
....
....

NOTES
....
....

6A 7 8 9 10 11 12P 1 2 3 4 5 6 7 8 9 10+

B=BREAKFAST   L=LUNCH   D=DINNER   S=SNACKS   R=RUN   E=EXERCISE

DAY 90

ARM ....

CHEST ....

WAIST ....

BELLY ....

HIP ....

THIGH ....

CALF ....

WEIGHT

BMI ....

MY RESULTS

DAY **1** DAY **90** DIFFERENCE

....	....	ARM	....
....	....	CHEST	....
....	....	WAIST	....
....	....	BELLY	....
....	....	HIP	....
....	....	THIGH	....
....	....	CALF	....

WEIGHT WEIGHT WEIGHT

BMI BMI BMI

....

NOTES

THIS PUBLICATION IS PROTECTED BY COPYRIGHT.

INDICATIONS ABOUT THIS AND MORE: ALL RIGHTS RESERVED. NO PART OF THIS PUBLICATION MAY BE REPRODUCED OR TRANSMITTED IN ANY FORM OR BY ANY MEANS, ELECTRONIC OR MECHANICAL, INCLUDING PHOTOCOPYING, RECORDING, OR ANY OTHER INFORMATION STORAGE AND RETRIEVAL SYSTEM, WITHOUT THE WRITTEN PERMISSION FROM THE COPYRIGHT OWNER. BRAND NAMES, TRADEMARKS AND REGISTERED TRADEMARKS USED IN THIS BOOK ARE THE PROPERTY OF THEIR RIGHTFUL OWNERS. THEY ARE USED ONLY FOR DESCRIPTION OR IDENTIFICATION OF THE RELEVANT COMPANIES, PRODUCTS AND SERVICES. RESBUTTNSIBILITY OF THE AUTHOR OR THE PUBLISHER, AND ITS AGENTS FOR PERSONAL INJURY, PROPERTY DAMAGE AND FINANCIAL LOSS EXCLUDED. FOR INFORMATION ON ERRORS OR AMBIGUITIES, WE ARE GRATEFUL TO ELIMINATE THEM IN FUTURE EDITIONS.

COPYRIGHT © GET FIT NOTEBOOKS
PUBLISHED BY: STUDIO 5519, 1732 1ST AVE #25519 NEW YORK, NY 10128
APRIL 2017, ISSUE NO. 1 [V 1.0]; CONTACT: INFO@STUDIO5519.COM; ILLUSTRATION CREDITS: © DEPOSITPHOTOS / @ PUSHINKA11 / © LZF

Printed in Great Britain
by Amazon